Top of the Morning

Worst First Sentence of a Novel

Selected by
Brian Edwards

National Radio

TANDEM PRESS

First published in New Zealand in 1999 by
TANDEM PRESS
2 Rugby Road, Birkenhead, North Shore City,
New Zealand

ISBN 1 877178 61 6

Design and production by Graeme Leather
Printed in New Zealand by Publishing Press Limited, Auckland

VARIETY-
The Children's Charity

In 1989 Variety Club of New Zealand was formed to raise funds and provide assistance for children aged 0–18 who are sick, disabled and disadvantaged. Since that time almost $6 million has been distributed to individuals and children's groups nationwide.

Variety operates a structured system of planned fundraising including the Countdown Variety Club Bash, Annual Gold Heart Appeal on 14 February, golf tournaments, movie and theatre premieres. Originally founded in the entertainment industry, Variety is known as The Children's Charity, and support is received from sporting and showbusiness personalities at fundraising functions and promotions throughout the country.

Assistance is provided to special needs children in the form of 52 Sunshine Coaches (Ford Econovans capable of taking fully laden wheelchairs or 12 able-bodied children), adapted trikes and bikes, holiday camps, books for schools and kindergartens, toy libraries and mobile ear clinics for the detection of glue ear. In addition, major donations of equipment have been made to several paediatric units at New Zealand hospitals.

INTRODUCTION

Brian stared at the blank computer screen in front of him, desperately trying to think of a witty introduction to the *Top of the Morning Worst First Sentence of a Novel Competition* compilation before 6 pm Thursday, the deadline set down by his draconian publisher, Bob Ross. The best idea, he thought, would be to make the first sentence of the introduction enormously long, containing everything he wanted to say, just like the entries to the competition itself.

Damn! Damn! Damn! That's already two sentences and I've barely even started.

Having decided that the best idea would be to make the first sentence enormously long and containing everything he wanted to say, Brian stared at the blank computer screen in front of him, trying desperately to think of a witty introduction to the *Top of the Morning Worst First Sentence of a Novel Competition* compilation, which contained the best entries from listeners to a competition on his high-rating Saturday morning radio programme.

Bugger! Left out the bit about the deadline and the draconian publisher. And no mention of National Radio or how long the competition has been running.

Having decided that the best idea would be to make the first sentence enormously long and containing everything he wanted to say, Brian stared at the blank computer screen in front of him, trying desperately before 6 pm Thursday, the deadline set down by his draconian publisher, Bob Ross, to think of a witty introduction to the *Top of the Morning Worst First Sentence of a Novel Competition* compilation, which contained the best entries from listeners to his high-rating Saturday morning radio programme on National Radio to a competition which had been running for the previous two months.

Oh no! Nothing in there about the standard of entries or the fact that royalties from the book will go to a worthwhile charity.

Having decided that the best idea would be to make the first sentence enormously long and containing everything he wanted to say, Brian stared at the blank computer screen in front of him, trying desperately before 6 pm Thursday, the deadline set down by his draconian publisher, Bob Ross, to think of a witty

5

introduction to the *Top of the Morning Worst First Sentence of a Novel Competition* compilation, the royalties from which would go to the Variety Club of New Zealand to help disadvantaged children, and which contained the best entries from listeners to his high-rating Saturday morning radio programme on National Radio to a competition, which the judges had said had been of a particularly high standard and which had been running for the previous two months.

Cripes! Forgot to mention the previous competitions or to thank a whole lot of people.

Having decided that the best idea would be to make the first sentence enormously long and containing everything he wanted to say, Brian stared at the blank computer screen in front of him, trying desperately before 6 pm Thursday, the deadline set down by his draconian publisher, Bob Ross, to think of a witty introduction to the *Top of the Morning Worst First Sentence of a Novel Competition* compilation, the royalties from which would go to the Variety Club of New Zealand to help disadvantaged children, and which contained the best entries from listeners to his high-rating Saturday morning radio programme on National Radio to a competition which had been running for the previous two months – the fifth such competition which the programme had run, the previous ones having sought the best limerick, excuse, short, short story and epitaph – which the judges had said had been of a particularly high standard, and, having managed at 5.59 pm precisely to cram everything in, realised to his chagrin that he had forgotten to thank Radio New Zealand, without whom there would have been no programme and no book, Paper Plus who had donated the prizes, the members of his little 'Top of the Morning' team (Catherine Saunders, Jane Dowell, Barry Hartley and Margaret Hancock), the aforementioned draconian publisher Bob Ross, whose 60th birthday party he had just recently attended, and his cats, Brandy and Benedictine, who had ripped up only five pages of the galley proofs, which, all things considered, Brian had thought was pretty good.

YES!!!

Brian Edwards, Auckland

WINNERS AND TOP TEN ENTRIES OF THE
TOP OF THE MORNING COMPETITION ARE:

'The white budgie!' screamed Ed, as the moon burst over the horizon and he opened the throttle of his 750cc Norton, the wind whipping long, blond hair across his face, and he saw with a blinding clarity that the way up and the way down were one and the same, a 6 was a 9 reversed, and Zen backwards was the French for nose; and all at once there he was gazing up at Miss Moir's oval face, trying to remember the first person plural of the imperfect subjunctive of *baiser*, and had he known then, as he knew now, the colour of the sound made by one hand clapping was a dark blue-green, he might never have read *The Magus* and run away to that *ashram* in Kathmandu and have there been vouchsafed the vision of the white budgie and would not now be rushing towards this consummation with the dark brown, scaly, ridged bark of the three-to-four feet in diameter trunk of the rapidly approaching macrocarpa.

Harry Ricketts, Wellington

Annie sighed as she opened a window to ventilate the room and wished that John's idea of scorning bourgeois convention would rise above and beyond the frequent and blatant breaking of wind.

Pauline Auger, Avonhead, Christchurch

We walked casually along the deck to the door, but what we didn't know was that the burglar was inside waiting to throw us off the balcony and the police would never find him (although his footprints were left behind).

Julia Caldwell (age 10½), Porirua

Should she clean both the toilets this morning or just one, then do the windows?

Jill Murphy, Prebbleton, Canterbury

Tonight, as I gazed across the floral carpet in our lounge room at my devoted husband Bert, gently snoring in his armchair, tummy full with a home-cooked meal of meat and veg, I decided to write a book about our life together – 40 years of wonderful memories, waking up, doing the housework, looking after the kids, eating tea and going to sleep – nothing more, nothing less, except for the occasional Saturday night snog, mmmmm.

Susan Alldred, Wellington

Warwick's lips curled in a wry, enigmatic smile as the strains of Tony Bennett's 'I Left My Heart in San Francisco' exploded through the quadrophonics of the Caddy's sound system, and he recalled with more than a little satisfaction that he had in fact left Gillian's spleen in San Francisco, her heart in San Diego, and her other vital organs in various locations throughout the Sunshine State.

Mike Edgar, Ponsonby, Auckland

If ever there was a woman who was unworthy of a single line, she was that woman, and yet, at first sight of her, for some inexplicable reason, I felt the sudden flow of ink in my pen.

Jim Edwards, Mission Bay, Auckland

She jiggled like a tea bag as he metaphorically poured cold milk into the boiling mess of her life.

Isobel Whooley, Plimmerton

Marty hated his neighbour with such a vengeance that each time he jumped the fence to pillage her plants, he also removed a pink plastic peg from her clothesline as a gift for his wife.

Christine Greene, Palmerston North

With rising horror, Derek the radio host realised that his Chinese takeaway was about to make a spectacular, unscheduled reappearance just as his long-awaited interview with Michelle Pfeiffer was getting underway in a small, airless studio totally devoid of any useful receptacles.

Pauline Auger, Avonhead, Christchurch

As the tongue of public inquisition probed deeper into the imbroglio, a melange of half-baked revelations and pseudo verisimilitude suffused the entire caucus, since every member had inserted an anxious finger into this seminal pie.

Barry Morrall, Palmerston North

Parboiled eyes head like a pumpkin splattering night juice among the guttered jetsam weaving gloriaward braincurdled dimly focusing on warm womb baths and scented oils minglematching memories of bluerobed gloria white skin under pertness thrusting armpits onion ripe and sweaty slimy cod smells gloria in excelsis todeo thy wont be done gloria your gombeen loverman coming to collect though briefly quandaried fresh morning dough smells of marlborough street panloaf awakening cravings the fourpence in his pocket could as readily satisfy (continues in similar vein for 775 pages)

Chris Wheatley, Titahi Bay, Wellington

The black buttocks of night sat moonless on the lawn.

Warren Thompson, Upper Hutt

14

Once upon a time in Toyland, Ned the wooden soldier with his bright red coat, shiny silver buttons and brand new boots of yellow, whipped a Mach 10 machine pistol out of his pocket and rained a hail of lead on his little friends screaming 'Die scum, die!'.

C Heywood, Kare Kare Beach

It was a clear and balmy night and the robber band were all tucked up in bed and the robber chief forbade Antonio to say anything.

Derek Belsey, Upper Hutt

Rory, handsome, hunkish and brimming with testosterone looked somehow uneasy as he adjusted his pink dress.

Tony Carton, Kaiaua

Among the 17 family members, friends and neighbours spread out in deckchairs, on rugs, or under trees in the Caldwells' large garden that summer afternoon were Roger Caldwell's third wife Tilly, Roger's second wife Jane's brother and sister-in-law Tim and Hazel Osborne, their twins Sam and Milly, Roger's step-sister Lucy and her best friend Kay, the three youngest Caldwell children Sandy, Chloe and Emma, Ann and Terry Simpson from next door, and Peter Andrews from the vicarage.

Helen Pennington, Palmerston North

Words, my life is words, pleading, persuasive, lying, shouting, embalmed in rejected manuscripts, so now I drown beneath this dross and as I drown I vomit up a final fountain of half digested words, mixed metaphors, and rusty clichés which will draw you deep into the maelstrom of my misery, and we will share, flashing before our eyes, a life thrice cursed.

Ian McKissack, Raglan

It was a sanguine day and the sun shone high in the celestial region like a great big yellow thing.

Bruce Collins, Kew, Dunedin

Myrtle Bagnall was a despondent woman, her husband a morose outcast, her children sullen and mentally impaired; nevertheless, she still wished to record their life together.

Dennis Wilson, St Johns, Auckland

As the blood red sun sank slowly behind the jagged peaks of the Sierra Nevada, inexorably, darkness fell.

Vera Robinson, Hamilton

If anything, it was the menacing sound of approaching thunder that provided a prelude to the unlikely success of Dame Appleby's Hawkes Bay millennium garden party, which had taken five years to plan and had exhausted all of her financial and social resources.

Dave Brown, Mt Eden, Auckland

Who, without a close examination of the neural theory to be presented in this text, could hope to unlock the uncharted mindscapes of seething emotion, the dark boiling pools of malice, the soaring pinnacles of ecstasy, the quiet gardens of tranquility and the raging desires that lurk beneath the exterior of the humble earthworm.

Mark Poletti, Lower Hutt

Jenny wept!

Janice Grace, Pakuranga

'Be gentle with me,' she cooed, leaning back into the shop doorway, as she expertly rolled the tight skirt up around her waist and hooked one five-inch stilletto heel into his hip pocket.

Frank Sillay, Wellington

Roger eased his lean yet strangely flaccid body into the cool grass and gazed with a kind of brutal tenderness into her large, limpid brown eyes, a tremor shaking his body as he ran his fingers through her tangled, blonde wool.

Mike Edgar, Ponsonby, Auckland

Rodney, flying Business Class across the Pacific for the first time, was most dissatisfied with the entrée of ratatouille.

Barry Morrall, Palmerston North

Evangeline Drake heaved her bosoms off the bar and, tipping the barman a raffish wink while adjusting her fedora, ducked out into the night.

Peter McConnell, Papatoetoe, Auckland

Insecurity squelched, then drowned my soul.

Jinine Duncan, Richmond, Nelson

When Inspector Murray arrived at the stately mansion to begin his investigation into the triple homicides, he was completely unaware that the old family retainer who greeted him at the door had committed all three murders.

Betty Livingstone, Palmerston North

One fine day, when the sun was shining and the bees were buzzing and the green grass was growing, a certain gentleman, Mr Brown, lay dying in his bed, his death rattle eagerly listened to by his greedy relatives who watched his immortal soul rise slowly from his navel up a single silver sunbeam and disappear into the smoke alarm which was set off, and the relatives got an awful fright.

Graeme Keall, Torbay, Auckland

Phillipa knew it was going to be a difficult evening when her husband returned home from work enthusing about the new heat exchanger he had designed that day, and totally failed to notice the benefits of the brand new fabric softener she had used on his shirts.

Jeanette Lange

With an expression of pure passion on his good-looking, manly face, Anthony, picnic basket and *lava lava* hung over his brawny arm, strode purposefully toward the lagoon where myriad stars twinkled and spun on its ink black surface, and Jennifer, her golden hair tumbling seductively over snowy white shoulders, her breath coming in short, anticipatory puffs, sat waiting under the caressing arms of a bounteous palm tree that shimmered in the moonlight.

Barbara Murison, Ngaio, Wellington

The train was late, so 21-year-old Christine's thoughts turned to the joys of modern bubble gum, as she looked in cross-eyed wonder at the great green beauty she had just produced when, without warning, the bubble, helped by a sudden gust of wind, burst, spreading its gummy greenness across her face, blocking the view of her fiancé stepping from the train, striding past her and disappearing into the crowd.

Jan Chisnall, North Canterbury

The book you are about to read is written by the one person who knows the truth behind Kennedy's assassination, the attempt on the life of the Pope, Norman Kirk's untimely death and who is Prince Harry's father – but that's another story.

Tonie Watts, Takaka

With a delicate pre-planned motion and excruciating finesse, he extruded 1.5 cm of the required specially-formulated substance onto the waiting implement, then, gazing soulfully into the mirror, opened the appropriate orifice and began to clean his teeth.

Garth Summers, Morrinsville

As I begin this, my journal, in this year of our Lord eighteen hundred and seventy-two, the stygian night is made ever more stygian by the all-pervading fog whose wraithlike tendrils envelop the city, and the only sounds are of the occasional passing hansom-cab, adding a muffled counterpoint to the scratching of your humble scribe's faithful nib across the vellum, but I am nevertheless uplifted, dear reader, by thoughts of the morrow, when I hie me to the docks, thence to embark on who knows what adventures on the bounding main aboard that fine vessel the *Marie Celeste*.

Bill Dengel, Christchurch

Dorothy Schwartz felt her innocent heart leap deep within her constricted bosom as Wayne, the grossly hirsute sportsjock who had recently moved into the next door apartment, now proudly wearing his sweats and slightly brown-stained sports socks, commenced a series of complicated somersaults and rebounds on his courtyard trampoline which began to squeak with an irritating rhythm, in tandem with her flushed heartbeat, wholly exacerbating an already anxious anticipation that something terrible would happen to Wayne if he should miscalculate his routine and come to grief on the hard cobbles before she could tell him of her all-consuming, eternal, passionate, yet unconsummated desire to jump with him.

Barry Morrall, Palmerston North

I am Miss Average.

Rose Lewis, Porirua

As a squadron of her chartered jets roared overhead, Christine Rankin, wild-eyed, legs akimbo, and wincing as her pendulous earrings beat a tortured tattoo against her throbbing cheeks, whipped the sweating horses, her chariot surging ahead in the Ben Hur stakes, while on the crowded terraces of the awesome amphitheatre her adoring workers danced and shrieked like frenzied dervishes in the satanic glow of the setting sun.

Don Evans, Roslyn, Dunedin

Random thoughts from his previous experience cluttered unbidden, unwelcome, unwanted into his fading mind – banana skins, ballpoint pens, eggshells, crushed snails, excrescence, baked potatoes, desire, vacuum cleaners, double bed duvets, Jenny Shipley – myriad minutiae melting magically into a foaming torrential porridge.

Garth Summers, Morrinsville

Posterity demands it, so here I begin the convoluted story of my life from, yes, even before I emerged from the womb, to the beginnings of illness in infancy, the gnomes in the hospital straight-jacket, finding everlasting love, the crunch of the Chev Impala, the snakes and bushfires, Sydney guns, the madwoman on the roof, to the joy of birth, of learning, of slow spiritual awakening … but more of this later!

Bronwyn Perry, Westland

There wasn't much left of Lothlorien after the goblins had ethnically cleansed the elves, torched their tree dwellings and turned the forest into wood chips, to be shipped to Japan and return as McDonald's chip wrappers, to be thrown from car windows and lie rotting in the gutter in Queen Street along with used condoms, vomit and broken glass.

C Heywood, Kare Kare Beach

Not since winning a Christmas turkey wishbone pull as a child had Arthur Sopwith known elation such as that which overwhelmed his senses as he read, and reread the interwoven, curlicued letters of his name on the certificate which proclaimed to the world that, against all odds, he was, at last, a fully qualified accountant.

Chris Wheatley, Titahi Bay, Wellington

With a blood-curdling scream Trevor plunged a butcher's knife into the frail heart of his silver-haired grandmother, which was uncharacteristic behaviour on his part, really, seeing that he grew orchids and had, at one stage, contemplated a career in the church.

Grahame Gillespie, Kelburn, Wellington

Jim Bennett approached No 11 Willow Place noting the bright orange front door, the paint, not at the terracotta end of the scale but a bright early morning California breakfast orange, creating an interesting juxtaposition of intense colour, contrasting with the red and yellow panes in the central leadlight panel which blended so well with the warm brass of the letter flap and door handle.

Robyn Gosset, Christchurch

All things considered and permitting himself the rare indulgence of a brief frisson of triumph, Rupert decided that the euphonium players symposium had been a resounding success, despite the embarrassing incident with Percival's mute which, together with the, as it transpired, fatal bone in his wife's creamed halibut, had caused a most unfortunate occurrence in the Matamata Metropole's Merrie Englande Eaterie.

Lois Davey, Invercargill

The summer night descended like some great cerulean duvet lowering on to an expectant mattress, and as I indulgently watched my hounds playfully rend the entrails of a young hare, my tender thoughts returned inexorably, inevitably, to Gillian, and that day in '38 when I first saw her at the house at Ruttingham Magna as she slid off her sweating Arab stallion, stroked his heavy flanks and ran along the terrace, her gay laughter setting the birds to flight in the rookery, whilst all the while her auburn tresses tumbled about her shoulders like nothing so much as molten toffee cascading down an alabaster escarpment.

Bill Dengel, Christchurch

Mist hovered over the swamp-like fetid dragon's breath as the moon struggled through the murky clouds, dimly revealing the wood's gnarled, bare branches like witches' hands at the throat of midnight.

Geoff Barlow, Remuera, Auckland

As the cacaphonic emanations from the antique Georgian doorbell reverberated along the ancient smoke-stained hallway, bouncing off the fake marble Greek colonnades and waking my dear companions the cockroaches, reclining in resplendent luxury under the Axminster carpet after feasting sumptuously on the carcass of the dead rodent I had maniacally crushed beneath my bare callused foot not more than an hour before, I limped Quasimodo-like towards the studded oaken door with the cast iron hinges that squeaked when it rained and the shiny brass knocker in the shape of Churchill's middle finger, the pain of the jagged 17-inch-long knife wound in my back racking my munificent yet oddly functional body with excruciating spasms and, wrenching open the door with an herculean jerk, muttered tremulously through bloody spittle-encrusted lips: 'No milk today, thanks.'

John Veal, Lower Hutt

He could hear the train whistle sounding closer, causing his thin black moustache to twitch in fury, as he struggled to hold the young maiden down on the tracks, mouthing, 'Curses, a thousand curses … is it left over right, or right over left?'

Peter Mitchell, Rakaia

It was midnight when Devina sat down to begin writing her first novel and, as she pondered for ideas, she heard the creaking of a gate … footsteps on the gravel beneath her window … and from the light of the moon saw a tall masked figure carrying a rifle … so, turning to her desk, she wrote, 'It was midnight when Rebecca sat down to write her first novel and as she pondered for ideas, she heard the soft creaking of a gate … footsteps on the gravel beneath her window … and from the light of the moon saw the tall masked figure, carrying a rifle …'

Nicki Waters, Napier

Gordon Hertzvooden, retired public accountant and world authority on military badges of the 19th century, threw aside a grey blanket of melancholy, rose from his bed of complacency, stepped into his literary trousers and, against the advice of friends, began to write the first page of his autobiography.

Peter Reid, Remuera, Auckland

Inspector Bett Schiffer, known affectionately within the force as 'Sniffer' for his unerring ability to nose out criminals, stood leaning against the railings of an Amsterdam bridge, perplexed for once by a particularly nauseous element in the foetid exhalations of the canal (a perplexity which would hound him for the next 200 pages), quite unaware that only minutes earlier, in the throng emerging from the Central Station he had brushed against a Frenchwoman of indeterminate age wearing that most aptly named perfume, 'Poison'.

Vera Robinson, Hamilton

'Where am I?' muttered Gerald inquiringly, unsure of his whereabouts after a night of unbridled revelry, until, rolling over, he spotted at his side a young beauty and knew in a flash, on the basis of her dusky skin, her tumbling mane of black hair and her proud features that bespoke the ancient mystical homeland of Hawaiki, that she was Maori, whereupon he whispered in her ear the words 'Kia ora', thereby demonstrating just how far Aotearoa New Zealand had progressed within a mere generation, given that his father, in similar circumstances, would not have had the cultural sensitivity to address the young lady in her native tongue.

Grahame Gillespie, Kelburn, Wellington

Wagner always brought out the best in Myrtle Higginbottom.

Pauline Auger, Avonhead, Christchurch

A rivulet of sunlight sparkled along the window sill like a gazelle springing across the veldt as Gunther, his heart still swollen with the transportation of bliss he had experienced when, in the satin of the night before, Gwendolyn had declared her love, emptied his prostate-strangled bladder of the Blenheimer that had demanded his urgent attention.

Mike Edgar, Ponsonby, Auckland

As Christopher Robin met the piercing eyes of his granite faced therapist, the wonder and innocence of his childhood leaked away and he accepted, gulping back his childish tears, the full pathology of his co-dependent, obsessive relationship with Pooh Bear, against the murky background surrounding the sinister symbolism of the empty honey jar.

Ian McKissack, Raglan

Whoever you are, whatever your family history and genetic profile, I urge you, dear reader, if you value your health, your state of mind, and the safety of your soul, to avoid reading this sentence at all costs.

Mark Poletti, Lower Hutt

Cynthia drove her off-white 1990 5-door 1300cc Toyota Starlet west along Victory Street and indicated her intention to turn south into Anzac Road, meanwhile checking to see that there was no vehicle approaching the corner from the west and signalling an intention to turn right, and at the same time that there was no driver approaching the intersection from the north and proceeding straight through to the south, since this was an uncontrolled intersection and she knew full well that she would be required by law to give way to any such vehicle or vehicles.

Grahame Gillespie, Kelburn, Wellington

It was only afterwards, as the destroyer rocked gently at anchor in Malta, and the crash of the ack ack and the numb terror of free fall faded like a bad dream, that Smyth noticed that sailors had rather lovely bottoms.

C Heywood, Kare Kare Beach

There was a marked cooling in the relationship between Rex King and his mother Jo when, against her express wishes, he changed his name by deed poll, officially expunging his first given name, Oedipus.

Chris Wheatley, Titahi Bay, Wellington

Joan lifted her eyes to the heavens while extending her arms to encompass the world as she knew it.

Craig McLanachan, Dunedin

David delivered the projectile vomit of his carefully arranged words with great force, and Sharlene met the toxic hail of venom with the same merry laugh that had sustained their relationship through the four days of their love.

Ross Elliffe, Picton

The skies opened as my car entered the southbound motorway at the Greenlane entrance and the rain slashed down in heavy sheets all the way to Huntly where it slowed to a persistent drizzle which in turn became intermittent with the occasional glimpse of blue sky as I drove through Ngaruawahia after which the clouds darkened again and discharged their loads with gusto through Hamilton until I drove into Taupo where I stopped for a cup of tea before continuing down the Desert Road in pouring rain with a threat of thunder in the air as I approached Taihape in time for a pie and coffee.

Mary Fisher, Napier

If it were not for the lank hair, acne pitted skin, hooked nose and troublesome overbite, Basil would have believed her to be the most beautiful woman he had ever met.

Helen Pritchard, Taupo

As the rhinoceros peered uncertainly through the wreckage of her front door, Mary sensed that this was to be no ordinary day.

Brian Creed, Levin

'Don't leave me!' Doris implored, her blonde hair suddenly unravelling in the surly wind like an egg exploding in a microwave oven.

Helen Brett, Opoho, Dunedin

Cynthia felt that Kurt had mud wrestled her feelings to the ground.

Tony Carton, Kaiaua

'I say, shall we stay with Sara and Simon in Sussex this summer for swimming, snorkelling, sunbathing on the sands and stacks of beach soccer?' lisped young Rupert excitedly from the balcony, as Sebastian hastily opened his umbrella on the pathway below.

Peter Beere, Takaka

Mary Jo had more than a broken heart; she had piles.

Tim Hambleton, Invercargill

After having ascertained the wording was PC, Lycestrata organised a supply of flyers be sent to many organisations including: IRN, NZPA, ARNZ, ACC, CYPS, CAB, DPA, NZBF, OUT, COPE, NZSO, AA, BNZ, SPUC, SFPOCTA, NZRU, WINZ, UNESCO, QANTAS, CORSO, WHO, et al.

Betty MacLean, Timaru

I slid the snub-nosed .38 into its chamois shoulder-holster and rescued the remains of last night's guacamole from the ice-box, spread it on three slices of rye and pushed them under the grill, carefully trimmed four slices of the Canadian bacon I get from the little deli on 33rd Street and threw them into a pan of hot fat along with two eggs, then sucked on a mug of hot java, as I considered what to do about the naked dead broad someone had dumped in my closet during the night.

Bill Dengel, Christchurch

Lord Henry Willoughby-Smith, the African explorer, slithered and lurched to the edge of the huge lake in the Sahara, but as he knelt to drink he failed to hear the hysterical laughter of Samuel Taylor Coleridge, the captain of the ship anchored not 50 metres away.

David Gibb Alexander, Mount Albert, Auckland

'Darling,' panted Paul, sinking into her lush, moist body, and grateful he had finally learnt not to call out specific names at climactic moments, when a combination of his obsession with fulfilling his body's lusts and a lack of visual clues to the identity of the co-operative female in the dark, had caused some difficulties in the past resulting each time in the need to find a new screw, 'of course I will never stop loving you.'

Claire Thompson, Awanui, Northland

Trudging in the mud by the pig pen, Jasper Hogwart tipped the last wheelbarrow of manure for the day onto the kitchen garden, stopping abruptly to drool as he sighted Miss Golightly, the governess, riding up to the manor in the Master's landau.

Geoff Barlow, Remuera, Auckland

Terrified, as Rodney, her jilted paramour, angrily began to cut through the locked door with a chainsaw, Monica lifted the handset and breathlessly jabbed 0800-HELP-FAST, which monotonously responded: 'Welcome to the urgent helpline … for ambulance emergencies, please press one … for civil defence emergencies, please press two … for fire emergencies, please press three … for police emergencies, please press four … for psychiatric emergencies, please press five … for traffic emergencies, please press six.'

Bob Kay, Lower Hutt

R. Hero was only three days old when the world ended.

Tony Girling, Clova Bay, Picton

Having never been known in the biblical sense or wanted by a woman, George felt grateful for his stamp collection.

Craig McLanachan, Dunedin

Reflecting upon my life, devoid of inspiration, barren of ideas, featureless as an invisible ink blot upon a blank white page, I surrender to the compulsion to record its full detail, dear reader, for your enjoyment.

Bruce Anderson, Riverhead, Auckland

'Is this the love that dare not speak its name?' murmured Biggles gingerly.

A Jane Read, Huntly

Barry sat on the finely grained custom made pine seat of his commode at 7.30 am on the dot, as his bowels had dictated every morning for the last ten years.

Brian D Falkner, Levin

Maxine hoiked loudly, and spat accurately at a passing dog, which stopped to lick off the viscous globule of orange mucous now streaked over its flanks.

Catriona Matheson, Otakou, Dunedin

Looking down on the Universe, He shook His head in despair and pressed the button.

Nicki Waters, Napier

The cat sat on the mat.

Mark Poletti, Lower Hutt

Hayley feigned surprise, throwing her freshly manicured hands behind her head and permitting a girlish whinny to escape her full red lips, for she knew that Garth would be watching from behind the Ottoman.

Peter Beere, Takaka

It was 11.53 on New Year's Eve, Friday 31 December 1999, the night before the dawning of the new millennium, and the men in their corporate suits, who had congregated in a corner of Bob and Jean's lounge, began cautiously loosening their corporate ties and unbuttoning the collars of their corporate shirts, as they earnestly expounded Y2K theories which would be proved one way or the other in the next seven minutes, while at the buffet bench of Bob and Jean's recently renovated kitchen the women, predominantly mothers, increasingly anxious, compared the provisions they had stored over the preceeding weeks – how many bottles of water, cartons of long-life milk, which brands of tinned peas, baby food, Irish stew, baked beans and sausages or spaghetti and meatballs – but Suzanne, glancing over to her nine-month-old daughter, asleep, oblivious, on Bob and Jean's plush pink couch – thankfully a tasteful old-fashioned deep rose pink and not baby-doll pink – congratulated herself for remembering to buy another hand-operated tin opener just this morning, to replace the one her eldest son had lost on his school camp last term.

A Barton, New Lynn, Auckland

Growing up in a small rural town in New Zealand had proved hard for Rangi, brutally beaten by his Maori father and the Catholic Marist brothers, and ignored by his alcoholic Pakeha mother, he had realised his homosexual tendencies early and had consequently been ostracised by his peers, alienated by both his cultures, angst-ridden, isolated from the homeland that part of his blood yearned for – unable to develop meaningful relationships with anybody, he had developed a deep feeling of inferiority and jealousy of anyone who 'achieved', he didn't think he could go on anymore and decided to kill himself in the dark oppressive night with waves crashing on the nearby shore, a fine mist wetting his face, his nostrils heavy with the smell of sand and salt, and his grandmother's pounamu pendant heavy around his neck.

Lucy Finlayson, Wellington

As she vacuumed the floor Charlene thought of the vacuum in her life.

Tony Carton, Kaiaua

The meal over, he licked cream luxuriously from his fingers and allowed his eyes to drift caressingly across the crisp white linen of the tablecloth to the woman he loved and his imagination to place his head in the silvery valley that marked the division between the white, pulsing mounds of her ripe breasts so that he could breathe deep of her muskiness, to savour the delicate saltiness of her body and for the steady thud of her heart to drown out the relentless tribal rhythms of the restaurant's resident dance band.

Alan Papprill, Glendene, Henderson

Gentle reader, I bring you my humble story happy, in the knowledge that this is the first time you will have ever read the autobiography of a field mushroom.

Claire Thompson, Awanui, Northland

Looking back at the cold, grey, featureless walls of the cruel prison that had been his home for these past five years as he was released on medical grounds after a lifesaving operation that resulted in the removal of part of his bowel, Archibald Preston – convicted fraudster, former English teacher and a grammarian of the strictest order – was irritated beyond measure that he had finished his sentence with a semi-colon.

Bryan McDaniel, Wellington

With startling proximity his eyes travelled down and over the table, over the remains of the meal they had just shared, over the small item of underclothing freshly laid there, then up and over the voluptuous body of his dining companion where, at the zenith of their gaze they met their match, crossed and set off down again, until finally he spoke, his voice extruding from his mouth in short crumpled pants 'I'll see your nickers,' he said, 'and I'll raise you my vest.'

Sean Joyce, Christchurch

The Scotsman reached under his kilt and produced his pride and joy, a likeness of Billy Connolly.

Craig McLanachan, Dunedin

Hamish Bond lacked his famous brother's savoir faire, preferring his cocktails stirred not shaken and occasionally succumbing to the temptation to pee in the bath.

Mike Edgar, Ponsonby, Auckland

I know you don't want to read this, but it's for your own good.

Anne Bowles

As Veronica looked forward to her wedding day, she wondered if the fortune teller's predictions would be right and that she and Graham would live in a three-bedroomed house, have lovely healthy children, travel to Australia for their holidays and, eventually, retire to the country where they would play golf and do 'Meals on Wheels'.

Nicki Waters, Napier

Myrtle inevitably wore purple, but today she sat in church in her usual pew, back row left-hand side, wearing a yellow knitted hat which, except for its curling black feather, was extraordinarily reminiscent of a tea cosy.

Maureen Doherty, Rotorua

It wasn't the best of times but it wasn't the worst of times, for although it was cloudy it wasn't raining, it was Thursday rather than Monday and the bus was only three minutes late.

Tony Girling, Clova Bay, Picton

The minister's approval of the application to introduce fish genes into potatoes gave Henry new hope that he could now renew his campaign for legislation of marriage between amoeba and plankton.

Roberet Tattershaw, Gore

'No' was not the answer she'd anticipated after asking wistfully, 'Will you still respect me in the morning?'

Kaye Lindsay, Christchurch

Gilbert Gobble knew every single word in the Concise Oxford Dictionary and as he sat on the porch in the midday sun he began to practise reciting them: 'a, aardvark, aback, abacus, abaft, abandon, abandoned, abase, abash, abate, abattoir, abbess, abbey, abbott, abbreviate, abdicate, abdomen…'

Tim Hambleton, Invercargill

There was something about the broad-beamed beauty sailing majestically through Auckland's crowded waterfront that evoked memories of a similar trim craft he'd once commanded, and he decided then and there to offer her a White House internship.

Chris Wheatley, Titahi Bay, Wellington

Glow of the Morning Mist searched her innermost psyche for that ephemeral glimpse of eternal truth which would lift her onto a metaphysical plane where she could forget she was also Maude Bottomley, aged 54, housewife, of Woodside Street, Epsom.

Claire Thompson, Awanui, Northland

As the chill waters closed over her head the whole of Tracey-Anne's wretched, accident-prone life flashed before her eyes – the housefire that had scarred one side of her face; the fall from the ferris wheel that had smashed her front teeth; the cricket ball that had pulped her nose; the dog attack that had taken a chunk from her chin – and now, just as she was recovering from the car crash that had fractured her skull, she leaned over the rail of the inter-island ferry to be sick, lost her balance and toppled into the icy depths …

Jenny Lynch, Lynfield

Paul was momentarily mystified when she offered him her dainties over the dining table but, after a moment's thought, he politely excused himself, made his way to the gents and, returning to his companion shortly after, murmured, 'Yes, they are a bit tight, aren't they?' as he handed her his.

C Daisley, Rotorua

As he rode across the prairie towards the Lazy B Ranch, a dozen red roses for Ellie May protruding from his saddle bag and his face tingling from Musk for Men aftershave with its vibrant fragrance of amber and incense enhanced by the earthy base notes of cactus and tumbleweed, Jed pondered again on the problems facing Sensitive New Age Man in the American West.

Joan Eddy, Christchurch

'Petulant, me?' Jocelyn snorted plangently as she strode purpose-fully out of the room, her arms pumping, lips pouting furiously and green eyes flashing with rebellion, as her raven hair spilled over her shoulders like an ebony cataract.

Peter Beere, Takaka

Jim felt that it was about time someone wrote a new critique on Adam Smith's *Wealth of Nations,* and he determined to attack it himself as he swung the manure-spreader into a sharp turn, skilfully missing the fence, as he drove down the paddock in a straight line, a satisfied smile on his face and the engine purring contentedly.

Lucy Finlayson, Wellington

'You done good, Sharlene,' Dwayne ejaculated nonchalantly.

MW Eade, Hastings

Santa was dead.

Claire Thompson, Awanui, Northland

Stung by the previous comment, Sophie sank into the turgid depths of a hysterical self loathing, immediately cancelling her pétanque lessons.

Craig McLanachan, Dunedin

As she melted into Jeremy's fond embrace, Jane was seized with an overwhelming urge to squeeze a ripened pimple she noticed on the back of his neck.

Carol Rankin, Wellington

'If chattels include everything that's been nailed to the floor or screwed to the walls,' muttered Rodney as he perused the Sale Agreement for his house, 'then you, Vicki, should be staying behind.'

Bruce Curran, Wanganui

How he overcame his sexual deviancy, how he conquered his innate violence, how he became successful, and how she came to love him can never be revealed.

Ross Elliffe, Picton

Immediately, if not sooner, John reached deeply inside himself and searched his inner man for any signs of an innate femininity.

Craig McLanachan, Dunedin

Henry's heart graunched like the worn-out gearbox of a 1930s Morrie 8 as he watched his long-misplaced ex-wife lurch drunkenly across the rain-moistened street, her oily reflection scattering about her like a badly assembled jigsaw puzzle.

Helen Brett, Opoho, Dunedin

Sue the vet had accepted with relish the dog's dinner of life thrown up for her until she met Hank the astronaut, who swept her off her feet before you could count to ten backwards, and sort of shoot up to a higher plane, like much higher up than the life she was expecting sort of, you know what I mean, sort of thing.

Tony Carton, Kaiaua

'Yes, yes, yes!' yelped Sandra as her hunky lover pressed freshly gathered flowers.

Craig McLanachan, Dunedin

Our story begins in late 1999 when the Ministry of Women's Affairs and the Human Rights Commission recommended to Parliament that the then Prime Minister's electorate be named Ashjenny for the months March to September inclusive and Ashburton for the remainder of the year, thus provoking outrage from the anti-smoking lobby.

C Daisley, Rotorua

Gordon 'Brownie' McPuce came to rue his decision to eschew his incontinence underpants in favour of a sleeker trouser line when later, on the dance floor, he cast a nervous eye at the lengthening queue for the loo, and, bowels rumbling, realised that, for this party animal, the party was over.

Bill Noble, Dunedin

The words 'or forever hold your peace ...' were scarcely out of the vicar's mouth before a pregnant woman with three small, dirty children hanging off her petticoat, a bewigged judge, a scout master in short pants, a one-legged pirate with a parrot on his shoulder squawking 'hello darling', a computer analyst, a woman in a gymslip flexing a cane, a jelly-covered female in a g-string leotard, a woman named Mrs Robinson followed by a young man in graduation garb, and an officer and a gentleman rushed forward to the front of the church.

Lynne Robinson, Hamilton

The competition to find the worst opening sentence to a novel was announced with little fanfare, conducted for the most part without incident and produced a mediocre result which was received on the whole with indifference.

Tony Girling, Clova Bay, Picton

Archie sat in his chair, looking out through the rain-streaked window at the graffiti-covered walls and litter-strewn gutters of the street, thinking of his childhood hopes and dreams and how they had all come to nothing, would come to nothing, how dreary day would lead to dreary day, until at last would come the solace of oblivion.

Bill Hartill, Titirangi, Auckland

I want to tell you a tale of the good old days when a man knew who his pals were and your door was left open all the time and folk were kind and true and we ate real Kiwi food and we all knew the name of the guys up and down the road in our town and kids were able to play in the park when the sun went down and a drug was what you took to fix the pain in your head when you'd had a skin full, a time when we all had a real job and Jim and me and Bill and Pete from next door had lots of cash to blow when we took off in our cars to have the time of our life in Gore.

Margaret Harraway, Christchurch

As the driver of the utility vehicle gazed despairingly at the cataclysm of horror which surrounded him, the nightmare of bloody and mutilated human and animal corpses, the desolation which could only be the destruction of Armageddon and the end of the world, he cried out against the fates from the depths of his tormented soul the only word which could express the unbearable agony twisting and distorting his devastated mind to the brink of madness – 'Bugger'.

Claire Thompson, Awanui, Northland

Charles hurried quickly in the direction of the gentle voice calling him from across the high walled garden, and in the far corner he saw that the large golden sunflower rising from behind the thicket of *euphorbia altisima* was now smiling at him.

Adrian Ellingham, Karori, Wellington

Barry had hoped to impress Sharon with an enthusiastic description of his new DOHC fuel injected, turbo-charged machine in canary yellow, but her slack jaw and glazed eyes suggested she had become hypnotised by the fluffy dice swaying gently from the mirror and he perspicaciously concluded that he would be pouring his heart out to no avail on the object of his desire, now slumped somewhat on the imitation tiger-skin velour seat covers and snoring ever so softly, and that he would gain more satisfaction from getting to work immediately on his big end.

F Wilson, Hamilton

Jay had what he described as a 'fatherly interest' in the girls from the Mickey Mouse Show, but Rhonda doubted that, as she watched him glued to the television screen, beads of sweat gathering beneath his thin grey hair, and a plump velvet cushion clutched tightly in his chafed slender hands.

Lucy Finlayson, Wellington

Richard menacingly squeezed Joan's face between his hands until her cheeks and chins dimpled into a strange concertina of pale fleshy dunes.

Helen Brett, Opoho, Dunedin

As the deep depression of life weakened and slowly moved away, a high ridge of hope centred itself over Shona and she prayed that for Grandpa, Nathan and herself it would mean blue sky, sunshine and not much wind, but the barometer was dropping and as the grey Holden turned into Forecast Lane, a cold front was approaching from the past.

Jim Hinkley, Inch Valley, Otago

Vladimir was really Pestov.

Tony Carton, Kaiaua

The limpid lake appeared as if it were a sheet of shining silver under a seamless sky mutating progressively to azure blue from the leaden pallor of dawn, and amid this scenic serenity the isolated angler drew up his rod with practised perfection and once more flipped it forward sending the snaking line whistling out like a graceful gossamer whip to place the artificial fly as tenderly as a tuft of thistledown into the pinpoint of one of several concentric circles resulting from the rising rainbow trout fleetingly feeding at the surface of the water.

Adrian Ellingham, Karori, Wellington

Fred Willowtree once played bowls against a man whose cousin's next-door-neighbour's doctor's best-friend's sister's lawyer's son was the next person to use a urinal after Bill Clinton the President of the United States; this is his story.

Tim Hambleton, Invercargill

The consultant rushed from one paradigm to the next, preceding each multimedia presentation with the one before it and following each powerful masterstroke with its successor in an expository display of position statements designed to disturb that stasis which inhibited quality and alter the firm's ethos so that it became changed and therefore different.

Ross Elliffe, Picton

As the soft evening mist insinuated itself dreamily over the hill, and the hazy sun sprinkled its benificent rays on the water like bright splatters of fat, Nirvana sighed gently, turned down the volume of his new Terry Oldfield CD, sipped a highly nutritious and verdant spirulina drink, and planned, no, dreamed, no, meditated on his next adventure, a spiritual journey into the deep, unfathomable oceans of his previous, ecstatic life as a dolphin.

Catriona Matheson, Otakou, Dunedin

Kylie Minogue, that Saturday night in Ashburton, the amazing double-jointed German Shepherd – could it all have been just a dream?

Peter Beere, Takaka

With her heart fluttering in her breast like a tiny imprisoned bird, gossamer tendrils of golden hair caressing the tips of her rosy ears and a blush mantling her damask cheeks, Diana was off for another riding lesson.

Brian Creed, Levin

Something had gone seriously wrong with the Reverend Smythe's train set.

Bruce Curran, Wanganui

Captain James Bigglesworth, DFC and bar, reclined in his leather chair, took a long drag on his cigarette, chugged a flute of Bollinger and began to ponder: Why on earth did Captain WE Johns give me such a ludicrous name?

Nick Bush, Brooklyn, Wellington

As well as being the secretary/treasurer of the Paeroa Bowling Club, Edith was also a keen gardener, but it was as a serial killer that a certain excitement entered her life.

Tony Carton, Kaiaua

The sound of a car backfiring disturbed Walter's concentration so much that he had to retrace his steps and start counting the cracks in the pavement all over again.

John Edgar, Christchurch

As Cheryl lay sleeping peacefully in her huge four-poster bed, in the inner city penthouse apartment she had bought after winning Lotto, her pedigree Persian cat, Mr Tiddles, padded softly into the room, jumped lightly on to the white duvet, walked up the bed and dropped a large slightly chewed rat's tail into her open mouth.

Tony Newport, Wellington

God's wrath had been building for some time.

John Benseman, Auckland

When he proudly showed her his crystal balls, Rebecca foresaw that marrying an economist had no future.

Bob Kay, Lower Hutt

Sarel awoke to the claustrophobia of stale breath.

Donald Crawford, Island Bay, Wellington

As the barmaid passed him his drink she said, 'There, that'll put lead in your pencil,' but he already knew it was her, not the drink, which would turn him from a 2B to a 3H.

David Black, Auckland

It wasn't that Brigit was important that made her important but the fact that she wasn't important that was important.

Ray Hambly, Napier

Gulls wheeled and screamed under an insolent gun-metal grey sky as Troy Davitt's sports car glided like a red corpuscle along the arterial route that connected Ventura with Santa Barbara.

Christopher Bell, Khandallah, Wellington

It is not my intent, dear reader, to bore you, but there are many things you need to know in order to comprehend the significance of my life.

Pat Rosier, Paekakariki

The eyes of the whole town, nay, the whole world were upon him today, as he battled, nay, grappled, nay, wrestled with the huge task ahead of him.

Lesley J Shaw, Wellington

'No signs of life here, ground-control, but it's damnably crunchy underfoot,' reported Commander Cody, oblivious to the tortured screams of ten million tiny souls, as he tramped back and forth across Alpha 5s' greatest metropolis.

Ron McGurk, Mt Albert, Auckland

Smoothing a gob of hair wax into his mop of already greasy curls, Ted took an extra moment in front of the mirror to admire his appearance in the new black jeans stretched so tightly over his crotch that nothing was left to the imagination and, with a self-assured chuckle, walked like a tomcat back out to the dance floor where all the chicky-babes were waiting for him.

Jenny Grimmett, Lower Hutt

Alamein Kopu, Tukuroirangi Morgan and Jack Elder, whose political party, 'Bright Light' held the balance of power for seven years in New Zealand tell their story of how they courageously put aside their differences to lead New Zealand out of the shadows and into the light.

Gina Garvey, Titirangi, Auckland

As the plop, plop, plop of the mud pool broke the dense silence of the Rotorua night, a body slid head first into its velvety depths as smoothly as an oyster down a fat man's throat, sparking five years of painstaking investigation into the shady world of adventure tourism before the geyser finally gave up its secret, tossing what remained of Harold Potts over his own Harvey-tiled roof.

Jennifer Ramshaw and Andrew Dreaver, Raumati South, Kapiti Coast

Fiona knew it was love at first sight when she saw a sad, sweet smile spread gently across his rugged face, crinkling his dimpled cheeks, until it reached his ears which began a rhythmic flapping motion in time with her beating heart.

Joseph Sparks, Wellington

This time Smith had definitely bitten off more than he could chew and found himself, having opened a Pandora's box, stranded between Scylla and Charybdis, his tail between his legs, and considerably deflated by this right-about-face of fortune, it being part of his optimistic temperament always to see the silver lining when others either gave up the ghost entirely, or after some futile chewing of the cud went off to eat the bread of exile overseas, a course of action deemed by Smith to be quixotic in the extreme, if not downright dangerous, a Sword of Damocles in fact, waiting to ambush the unwary.

Kathleen Mayson, Wanganui

Just as the lady bowlers sat down to afternoon tea, Beryl gave a deep sigh, raised her pencilled eyebrows skywards, clutched at her throat and, with a desperate whimper, sobbed, 'I know we've had a lovely day's bowling and it could be because it was a mixed gala, but I can't help it – I just want a man!'

Judy Lowe, Melrose, Wellington

thats real cool man   that teacher jerk knows somefing and stuff arter all man   said not to waste his time marking essay and stuff man   send it to top of morning and stuff man   some dude edwards wants worst sentences and stuff man   teacher jerk says im a natural says must win money and stuff man   real cool man i needs money and stuff for a fix man

Alan Williman, Christchurch

When the phone rang Gerald wondered who it was.

Nicki Waters, Napier

PJ, an SCPO in the RN, revved up his BSA and sped to his meeting at DHQ with JK, a PO on an MTB.

Toni Cathie, Albany, Auckland

Bill dialed the 0800 number, waited a minute before getting a connection, then, after listening to a period of musac, heard the taped message and pressed with interspaced pauses, three then five, followed by six, to obtain details of his account status.

Trevor Betts, Naseby

Catching cholera at the right time was not something Christopher engineered but was purely serendipitous.

Ray Hambly, Napier

Sitting on the side of the huge bed, next to the gently snoring American with the steely grey hair, Sheryl, a buxom 28-year-old brunette with a double major in English and Political Science from Victoria University pondered, as she quietly pulled on the expensive black lace panties bought especially for this night, the exquisite irony in the fact that her bid for the presidency of the Wellington Central branch of KOMP (the Keep Out the Multinationals Party) would probably depend upon this, the second night of the APEC meeting here in Auckland.

Betty Irons, Palmerston North

Eunice paused, adjusting her horn-rims absent-mindedly with one hand, toilet brush poised precariously mid-flight in the other, a wistful smile playing softly on her lips, as she recalled that memorable first summer with Cyril when they holidayed in Gore.

Cathy Middlebrook, Auckland

'Stand and deliver,' said the dark clad figure to the legless beggar, for he was a cruel and heartless man.

Sven Christensen, Mornington, Dunedin

Reginald contemplated his navel swimming in a sea of pink flesh above the low-slung line of his magenta togs and decided he was a man who could grace any calendar.

Carol A Cooper, Lyall Bay, Wellington

The deep theological implications of the breakdown of the demarcation between successive phases of the diurnal cycle that was manifest in the high latitudes of the austral regions during the festive season were not immediately obvious to Cyril, but he did have to admit that singing 'Silent Night' in the midnight sunshine seemed a little strange.

John Edgar, Christchurch

'Love and marriage go together like a horse and carriage' had long been the motto, nay the rule of thumb of the Montmorency family, but for the ravishing Kyleigh to have joined in holy matrimony with the concave-chested, lily-livered, round-shouldered, knock-kneed, pigeon-toed Harvey Harrison-Smith, was more than the family had ever dared hope for.

Lesley J Shaw, Wellington

Despite her objections, Robert was fairly sure that Millie would maintain his stamp collection after he had gone.

Warren Palmer, Dunedin

On the morning my budgie died I burnt the porridge.

Josie Buchanan, Tauranga

Natasha stretched languidly in the Alpine sun and watched, fascinated, as a symphonic puff of breaking wind gently stirred a Mexican wave into the tall colours of the surrounding wildflowers.

Barry Bain, Arrowtown

As he lay gasping on his death bed, his body wasted by the ravages of time and indolence, old Bill wondered whether his life might have been better if he'd been brave enough to talk to girls.

Warren Palmer, Dunedin

It is clear to anyone that if a Maori man and a Maori woman engage in, well, physical relations, this may result in the birth of a Maori child, but if, well, physical relations between a Russian man and a Chinese woman resulted in the birth of a Maori child, it would have to be through a longer, more convoluted and altogether more subtle chain of cause and effect – a chain of cause and effect which you, dear reader, may already have realised, contains within it the germ of a solution to the eternal paradox faced by tax accountants in most provinces of Brazil.

Ben Glass, Te Aro, Wellington

After hearing the priest's words, 'I now pronounce you man and wife, you may kiss the bride,' Oscar turned towards his beloved, lifted the veil and to his horror found himself staring at the mocking eyes and triumphant smile of the woman he had expected would be his mother-in-law.

Wendy Anderson, Karori, Wellington

Ingrid secretly enjoyed the night-time frolics with her neighbour's garden gnome.

Josie Buchanan, Tauranga

Fame was indeed no stranger to Mary Lou, having in her youth been crowned Miss Spring Blossom 1959 in her hometown of Toadsuck, Arkansas.

Cathy Middlebrook, Auckland

After peering furtively from dingy grey blankets, the sun suddenly sprang into full view, brazenly flaunting his golden nakedness, while bashful clouds blushed prettily against the sky's shocked pallor.

Iris Melville, Dargaville

The circumlocution necessary to obscure by periphrasis the nomenclature of the miscreant who by subtle imputation insinuated that my literary composition was extravagant verbiage is without exculpation and, in amplification, I would vouchsafe that the ineptitude of his comprehension is caused by the paucity of his vocabulary and so deign to controversy his preposterous presumptions but you, my dear reader will, I am assured, comprehend without difficulty.

Jean Muir, Warkworth

It was one of those nights after work, you know the way it is, you work hard, play hard, just a group of decent jokers, Trev, Murray, Wayne, Scott, down at the club, footie on the telly, the missus at home cooking some tucker, when some bastard comes over to our table and starts talking about postmodernism and the problem of the anomie, loss of identity, direction, roles, the attack of the male sexual ethos, so we took the hint, went into the toilets, changed out of our dresses, washed off the mascara, put the stilettos back in the lunch boxes and went home and thought thoughts about sheep drench, V8s and Rugby, but we'll never forget that night, especially since we were banned from the club forever.

Tony Carton, Kaiaua

As she examined her thighs with the aid of a magnifying glass, a horrified gasp escaped Melynda's collagen enhanced lips and she sank to her knees praying, 'Please God, not cellulite.'

Iris Melville, Dargaville

Blake looked around him and realised how much he had come to love this wild and untamed land and, as he turned his strong, determined jaw to the dark, throbbing sky, dripping with promise, he felt infinite sorrow at the void without Courtenay and he knew then that she was his woman, the she to his he, the her to his him, the mother of his unborn sons.

Karen Stevens, Wellington

As he stood there chewing thoughtfully on a slice of haggis, Tam O'Shanter tipped at a jaunty angle, plaid arranged tastefully over one shoulder, hairy tasselled sporran dangling at the front of a Royal Hunting Stewart tartan kilt; 'I can see where you're coming from,' I quipped.

John Neave, Hamilton

The notes from the piano rippled through the house, pianissimoing along the windows, crescendoing down the stairs and allegroing into every niche and corner, filling the heads of the other residents with thoughts of murderous intent, directed towards whoever it was suggested Christobel should take piano lessons.

Robyn Gosset, Christchurch

Fed up after years of struggling with such a difficult problem, many of the parents of 2.5 children gathered together for the purpose of joining these disparate halves, only too aware that some were halved horizontally and some perpendicularly, and that ownership of the resulting whole would be decided by the toss of a coin.

Irene Swayn, Napier

Upon hearing the postman's shrill twin-pea whistle echo around the mews, Emile Windermere emerged from her scented tub, and being of shy and modest disposition in such circumstances, dared not venture to open the studded oak entry door as was her custom, but knelt instead on the floral shag-pile in order to better observe the approaching courier through the filigreed brass flap as the low morning sun beamed through the bevelled stained glass and sent warm shimmering prismatic slivers of spectrum colours over her wet olive skin, now rising in goosebumps at the expectation of the embossed envelope about to fall into her trembling suppliant hands.

Barry Bain, Arrowtown, Otago

Cyril Searle's Sundays ceased to have meaning after God died, but macrame helped fill the void.

Chris Wheatley, Titahi Bay, Wellington

With the carelessness of youth, Jason spat in the face of fortune, vomited into the lap of destiny and blew his nose on the tapestry of life.

Tony Carton, Kaiaua

Norman Bicklesthwaite, a 50-year-old bachelor, often went to the ballet, not to admire the skill and grace of the dancers or even to enjoy the music, but simply to feast his watery eyes on the female dancers' legs.

John Halliwell, Motueka

When Gladys told him she no longer loved him, Horsefall displayed all the classic symptoms of rage – sweating, pallor, palpitations, erectile dysfunction and testicles withdrawing into his lower body cavity.

Reg Tomkins, Wainuiomata

'Strewth!' exclaimed Basil, endeavouring to look both flabbergasted and senatorial while trying desperately to control a sudden onslaught of inopportune flatulence, 'Strewth!!'

Murray Robb, Tawa, Wellington

Gerald had always been concerned with the minutae of his life so, on the day he decided to write his autobiography, he pulled on his grey windcheater with the frayed red cuffs, double locked the back door of his rented house and strolled the 90.6 metres to his local bookshop, where he bought ten topless A4 pads ruled in green, 6 red HB pencils, one eraser, two pencil sharpeners and a metre-long plastic ruler.

Hilary Ramshaw, Clive, Hawkes Bay

Josie had a strong premonition that something bad was about to happen to her, so, instead of driving the 50 kilometres of busy highway to her mother's place, she locked her car in the garage and opted instead for a leisurely bath, with her old valve radio perched on its rickety shelf above, playing soothing music.

VF McGunnigle, Christchurch

Had he known that aliens, microscopic by Earth standards, had landed in his hair, Ted might not have scratched his head at that precise moment, thereby denying the world the accumulated wisdom of an enlightened civilisation which the Alpha Bacterians had travelled 12 billion light years to bring us.

Chris Wheatley, Titahi Bay, Wellington

Carefully Unshaven Matthew grinned brutishly as he gunned his new boat Hooter Patrol into the Hauraki Gulf.

Mike McCree, New Lynn, Auckland

The trainspotter, huddled miserably beside the tracks in the icy rain, pulled his anorak closer about him, and removing his spiral-bound notebook from his damp pocket, was depressed to find that his last entry, made almost four hours ago, had smudged figures so as to be unreadable.

Rose Isdale, Christchurch

As she examined the knife, Josephine said, 'But Henry, you had sex last leap year and today's only January.'

G Soanes, Flagstaff, Hamilton

As Rodney Postlethwaite stood at the end of the platform, dressed in a beige anorak, hand knitted jersey, crimplene trousers and sandals, the last rays of the evening sun glinting on his thick tortoiseshell glasses, he realised, too late, that he already had the number of the diesel engine that was bearing down on him.

Sarah Thompson, Whitby, Wellington

'Bollocks,' said God, 'that's what we'll call them.'

Cliff Alexander, Taupo

As Alice walked away, the image of two bowling balls bouncing on a trampoline came into Bernard's head and he felt compelled to turn and follow her.

Frank Nerney, Helensville

94

Sophia Sogood gasped as she admired her reflection in the window of the Down Stuffing bedding shop and noticed that Maria Goodman was doing the same thing in the window of the Nip and Tuck boutique for mature ladies opposite, which meant that, horror of horrors, she could see Sophia admiring her reflection across the street.

Tony Broome, Christchurch

Mary gazed transfixed at the spectacle in the garden beneath her window, for there on the red geraniums, gliding slowly closer, closer, were two pubescent snails, their hormones obviously near raging point.

Iris Melville, Dargaville

Drusilla Grey lowered her cornflower blue eyes, so that her silky lashes lay in perfect arcs on cheeks rosy with nothing more than health, pushed back the nut-brown hair from her clear, untroubled forehead in a gesture that was demure yet seductive, sensing, as she stood on the terrace of this villa overlooking the Mediterranean with her new employer, Rafe St John Sternheart, the tall, dark, saturnine man who now looked at her with disdain, that the two exuberant children she had been engaged to care for, would come to love her, just as she would love them, that she would misunderstand the nature of Rafe's relationship with the beautiful, tempestuous Contessa Francesca del Imbroglio, his present house guest, but that on a future night under liquid stars and a luminous moon, on this very same terrace, he would sweep her into his arms, crush her to him, press his lips to hers, saying that she was a silly little goose, and that he had loved her from the first moment he had laid eyes on her; and that after he had released her from his passionate embrace, she would gasp, 'Sorry, but I don't dig men!'

Janet McRae McDonald, Maori Hill, Dunedin

He looked like a rabid dog, all saliva and wild eyes.

DS Shadick, Howick, Auckland

Murgatroid, Gertrude McGillakuddie's sister, was secretly beside herself when she discovered that Ethel, her son Cecil's wife, had begun an adulterous relationship with Percy, the son of her ex-lover Berty Throggmortin, thereby creating the opportunity to instigate her wildest fantasy, the Murgatroyd and Ethel McGillakuddie/Percy Throggmortin *ménage à trois*.

Brian D Falkner, Levin

Rodger's seasonal allergy was such that any spontaneous evacuation of mucus from his nasal passages rendered his handkerchief completely unfit for any future use.

John Edgar, Christchurch

The first cutting of the hay paddock revealed much wildlife, including Mr Fitzgerald the solicitor and shapely Miss Smithers, who were both deeply involved in an investigation of the reproductive process of the Sussex Lesser Nude Nymph.

G Soanes, Flagstaff, Hamilton

'Darling!' swooned Madeleine Crudd in the arms of the heir to a publicly listed multinational communications, financial and advertising empire who had been granted a unique package of 2.3 million ordinary share options at an extremely attractive discount, as she caught her spindly heel in a loop of her brand new snow-white pile carpet, and catapulted her prized Harrods crystal flute of genetically unmodified tomato juice, extracted expressly for this romantic encounter, across said carpet in a spirographic swathe.

Murray Robb, Tawa, Wellington

Watson knew that trypsin is formed in the intestinal lumen from the inactive trypsinogen fibrin generated at the site of blood clotting from the inactive fibrinogen, but he was buggered if he was telling that smart arse Holmes the exact cause of death.

Chris Wheatley, Titahi Bay, Wellington

As she sheltered in the doorway, snuggled into the rough tweed of Bob's jacket, Agnes was strongly conscious of the feeling of newness of the engagement ring on her third finger left hand, but only dimly aware of the gentle slopping of the passing night cart that would all too soon feature so prominently in her life.

Joanne Simonson, Oamaru

My name is Bobbi-Lou, Miss Dry Gulch in the US of A and I am 17 years old, and my hobbies are buying clothes for me, and painting with numbers and saving all the poor people in the world and this is my story.

Mary Ashford, Masterton, Wairarapa

Roscoe, who had spent the pre-dawn hours counting each of his breaths and calculating how many he had left before they took him to his appointment with the hangman, watched with trepidation as the pallid orb of the sun rose inexorably from behind the bank of clouds which hugged the eastern horizon like grey blankets on a rumpled bed and lit the flat, featureless prairie with a thin, watery glow, and pondered, as he heard the sound of footsteps approaching, whether there might not be a drop of rain later on in the day.

VF McGunnigle, Christchurch

Mrs Jenkins tried to reassure herself that her teenage daughter's new habit of dressing in a very sexually provocative way was a manifestation of a normal stage of life, as indeed puberty had been identified as a critical stage in the development of a person's unique identity (Erikson, cited in Smith, 1998, pp 201-206) and that typically in adolescence allegiance shifts from the family to the peer group especially in highly visible areas like dress (Hoogstraten, Blostein, et al, 1988, p 21) and moreover she was aware that some neo-Vygotskian theorists have stated that the child 'is not a passive recipient of guidance but is actively involved in transforming knowledge', a process known as 'guided reinvention' (Tharp and Gallimore, 1972, p 37), but she was also worried that Sue was becoming a tart.

Tony Carton, Kaiaua

She was a magnet to his steely gaze, and he was riveted.

Ron McGurk, Auckland

As she stood in the dock giving her evidence, Virginia described how she had watched in fascinated terror as the huge and repulsive cockroach climbed slowly up and over her husband Arthur's shiny dewlaps, heading straight for his open mouth, and knowing that this was only a dream, seized the baseball bat kept alongside the chamber pot under the bed and smashed the evil creature to a pulp.

Margaret Harraway, Christchurch

Ross was still unsure in his own mind as to whether Einstein's General Theory of Relativity was an ontological or an epistomological view of the nature of reality, but then it hardly seemed important as he watched his new bride undress on their wedding night.

John Edgar, Christchurch

Norman Frigworthy was a character best forgotten.

Michael Smith, Otahuhu

As Ralph dipped his wine biscuit into his morning cup of coffee, there was a noise just like a thunderclap in the construction yard and he was absolutely astounded to see the yellow portaloo collapse in a pile of plastic, leaving Buckets Thompson standing there with his trousers about his knees and clutching the racing section of the *Daily Telegraph*.

Neroli Cottam, Dunedin

Henry felt unable to move when the younger Miss Brackenbridge sat on him.

G Soanes, Flagstaff, Hamilton

The tense fusiliers stood up to their knees in the stinking mud of the trenches, listening to the machine-gun fire rat-tat-tatting like a percussionist who had lost his way in 'Bolero', and waiting for the order to advance from one hell to yet another.

Barry Bain, Arrowtown, Otago

With the benefit of hindsight it was obvious that Lady Maud was really Max von Grottheimer in drag and that he'd murdered Sir Algernon in the sauna with the cast iron lawn dog in order to gain control of Bogshaw Manor's vast oil reserves which he'd learned about during his torrid affair with Mystery ffanshawe, Sir Algernon's first wife's lesbian lover, leaving just one question unanswered: where exactly did Bogshaw Manor get its silly name from?

Chris Wheatley, Titahi Bay, Wellington

Such a wind, a wind of malice and pain, born in the distant ice fields far to the south, whipping the sub-Antartcic waves to a frenzy as it screamed its derision at the ocean, a wind to crash against the coastline and break the beaches to submission, to tear through the pines surrounding the southern cemeteries, rattling the boxes of the pioneers even in the depths of their rest, a wind to scour and ravage, to rip the corrugated iron roof from the old shearing shed and spin it slamming against the new farmstead, a wind to remind the civilised city swank that for all his shelter there was lurking just beyond his senses an untamed, bitter world; a wind to disrupt the best and worst of city life, to dislodge the off-bail just as the fast off-break missed the stumps, to swirl the schoolgirl's skirt so that a gentleman had to look everywhere except where he wished; but a wind that made absolutely no impact upon the bald pate of Jack McTavaunt as he waited at the bus stop in George Street for his trip home at the end of another working day.

Warren Palmer, Dunedin

At the end of the day as Corey carefully lowered himself down onto the couch beside the potatoes he gazed through the window of opportunity and onto the level playing field, all the while wondering if the cause of the incipient ache in his innards was groin strain, a case of tall poppy syndrome, the result of his recent fall from the corporate ladder or if he was already in the clutches of the Y2K bug?

Bronwen Gunn, Blenheim

When Mary decided to scale Mount Flooster (2000 m, 6561.7 ft), she expected to carry a pack weighing 80 lb (36.287 kg), with a total of 3250 gm (112.88 oz) of dehydrated food for nourishment, and she fully anticipated having to purchase new climbing boots (size 9, size 11 American, six 10 British, size 13¾ Japanese).

Warren Palmer, Dunedin

Although I didn't realise it at the time, the best advice my mother ever gave me was to wear clean underpants when making a rail journey.

Sandy Winterton, Melrose, Wellington

Only after he had carefully sharpened his scalpels and arranged his instruments with precision upon the stainless steel tray, did Julian allow his mind to fill again with the almost erotic excitement he always felt at the thought of the first incision he would soon be making in the cold, pale body before him, fresh from the morgue.

Diana Parsons, Christchurch

For a long time now I have been going to bed early.

Alfred Sneyd, Hamilton

Who among us, if we are totally frank, can honestly say that we have not had the occasional sexual attraction towards pigs?

Tony Carton, Kaiaua

Each performance night, after hand washing them each three times, 84-year-old Petriska dried the tights belonging to the National Russian Mens' Ballet company by covering her naked self in them, and letting her not insubstantial body heat do the rest.

Gina Garvey, Titirangi, Auckland

It was a cold, wet summer, but Percy the Pine still managed to grow 35 centimetres before autumn set in.

Warren Palmer, Dunedin

Smith washed his hands six times before the third closet from the right in the Paddington Station unisex became free, and then lifting the seat, wiped the toilet rim with the special formula to reveal the message: 36 Western Ave, Golders Green, Tuesday 3 pm, Ninotchka, PS, don't forget to close the seat.

Alec Rainbow, Havelock North

The cockroach died the instant the newspaper struck, but its hatchlings stirred grimly, knowing their time had come.

Julian Heyes, levin

Sketchly rubbed his cereal-coated beard as he gazed out the window, wondering what his new neighbours might think about a clothesline carefully pegged with undies that defied gravity and bras that would have boosted anyone's confidence.

Diana C Mead, Whangarei

After several minutes' wrestling with his more sensible instincts – nay! his entire upbringing! – Gordon opted for the flashy multi-coloured paperclip assortment over the staid stainless steel ones, insouciantly flung the packet on the checkout counter, and inwardly hummed the opening bars to Jim Morrison's exhortation to 'break on through to the other side'.

Bill Noble, Dunedin

With a fluttering heart, Priscilla watched the savage, handsome figure push the old lady into the path of the passing lorry, knowing that even though he had destroyed her company and the lives of its workers, abandoned his former wife to sharks in the Bay of Bengal, sold radiation-contaminated cordial to third world countries and napalmed many villages of defenceless children, deep inside he was still that gentle and vulnerable child she had once known as 'Spotty' McPherson.

D Tan, Stratford

T'was the grimmest minute of the foulest hour of the darkest day of the vilest month when Black Ned Strawkins was born to a filthy hag in a fetid hovel in the execrable village of Stenchcombe in the loathsome year 1863.

Sandy Winterton, Melrose, Wellington

The furry brown opossum gazed thoughtfully with its large brown unblinking eyes at the intense beam of light that was directed at him and ruminated quietly as to what this light might signify.

Steve Wyn-Harris, Waipukurau

Emma counted her children one last desperate time, cursing both her Catholic husband and her own shortcomings in numeracy.

Julian Heyes, Levin

As the screaming bristles bit deep, demolishing bone, arteries and cartilage and liquidising internal organs like a food processor, Bradley knew in his last living moments that he had made a significant error of judgement in calling the guy with the electric toothbrush a 'weird-looking dork with an attitude problem'.

D Tan, Stratford

His BMW hidden discreetly under the moonlit trees, Dr Morrison embraced Sally in the unlit entrance to the Nurses' Home, but as she stared into those wonderful bedside manner eyes, she wondered if she should mention that recently her genital area had become very sensitive, easily irritated and intensely itchy; and that it was also sore and dry and she had begun to find bladder control difficult.

Terry Chapman, Waiatarua, Auckland

He was tired of Italian, in fact so terribly tired after a fortnight travelling by Goliath down the front of The Boot, that he knew the very next time he stopped in the last coastal village before dark … pressed wearily in from the street through the bead drape … to be confronted by the ubiquitous red gingham cloths and curtains and those execrable chianti bottles bunged with creamy candles slumped like osteophytes around old vertebrae … that suddenly he would just have to kill – and kill brutally – whosoever happened to smilingly proclaim, yet again, how indeed fortunate he was that very evening, of all evenings, to find the osso buco on special!

Gerald Turnbull, Epsom, Auckland

Everybody was surprised when 98-year-old Texas billionaire, Tex Ewing's 18-year-old wife, Tiffany, died of a heart attack on the night of their honeymoon.

Edward Johnston

After four years of rigorous and celibate instruction in the Seminary, Reginald Thornbury, drably garbed in the rough robes of a Tibetan novice monk and now known only as Xavier, his worldly possessions in a calico bag roped over his shoulder, alighted from the Orient Express, his last contact with the western world severed at this small flag-station in the Himalayan foothills, and as he paused for a moment to raise his hood against the chill wind sighted the most gorgeous woman he had ever set eyes on, smiling at him through the dining car window with a slender brown braceletted arm resting elegantly on the sill and a bubbling flute of Louis Roederer raised in long bejewelled fingers, bidding him reboard the train.

Barry Bain, Arrowtown, Otago

As Ernie lowered himself into the sewer, he was reassured to know that his job was secure for the rest of his life.

Arthur Jones, Little River

If the banana was just at the right stage of ripeness, Edwin found he could push most of it through the gaps in his teeth before it collapsed.

Marguerite Wade, Hillcrest, Auckland

It seemed to him to be a contradiction in terms to use skill and literacy to compose a worst first sentence when, after all, the sentence wouldn't be the so-called worst sentence unless it conveyed some degree of cleverness, wit and imagination, even perhaps poetic resonance, so after agonising over the matter for several weeks, he decided, notwithstanding his competitive nature, not to enter the competition and turned for solace to a cup of hot milky coffee and his well-thumbed copy of Dante's *Inferno*.

Michael Wright, Devonport, Auckland

As Stacey-Lou sashayed like a plover towards her lover around the decaying body parts and fresh road kill in the Splatter Suite, she marvelled at the lengths the staff at Mangaweka's newest tourist attraction, Gary's Gruesome Theme Hotel, had gone to to make their honeymoon real choice.

Alison Murray, Wilton, Wellington

The day that Lady Agatha de Villiers-Smythe discovered from an anonymous correspondent that her real father was a Harrogate fishmonger, she cancelled all her Mayfair social engagements and booked the first flight to Buenos Aires, with the intention of reuniting with her gaucho lover whom she had met on her husband's diplomatic tour of the pampas the previous year.

Geoff Barlow, Remuera, Auckland

Robin Jangswaites' badly mutilated, beheaded body was discovered in Monsignore Noir's bat-ridden wine cellar the same Sunday before Lent that socialite Amanda Fullers-Purm slipped on a wet mullet, dislocating her pelvis, causing The East Wrexham Amateur Theatre Group to cancel the opening performance of 'Oh Calcutta'.

Ralph Baré, Palmerston North

'I understand where you're coming from, and it's a big ask,' the literary editor explained, 'but we're very much state of the art here, and even though I hear what you're saying, I think at this particular point in time we should be up at the sharp end, getting our heads around the problem and pushing the envelope, so that we can get this show on the road, tread the thin blue line and, at the end of the day, start talking serious money.'

Barbara Newburgh, Christchurch

Index of Contributors